Go Programming

Make it Easier with Step by Step Guide
Step Guide
*Unofficial edition

By Donald Mackey

Table of Contents

Disclaimer

While all attempts have been made to verify the information provided in this book, the author does assume any responsibility for errors, omissions, or contrary interpretations of the subject matter contained within. The information provided in this book is for educational and entertainment purposes only. The reader is responsible for his or her own actions and the author does not accept any responsibilities for any liabilities or damages, real or perceived, resulting from the use of this information.

The trademarks that are used are without any consent, and the publication of the trademark is without permission or backing by the trademark owner. All trademarks and brands within this book are for clarifying purposes only and are the owned by the owners themselves, not affiliated with this document. **

Introduction

The Go programming language is known for its ease of use. One can accomplish more just using a few lines of code, as opposed to other programming languages in which too much coding is needed. Anyone can learn how to program in Go, including those with no knowledge regarding programming. All you need to have is an interest in learning how to program in Go. This book is a guide for you to learn how to do this. Enjoy reading!

Chapter 1- A Brief Overview of Go

Go is a programming language whose syntax is similar to that of C programming language. The language is statically typed. Google released the initial version of the programming language in 2007. Some of its unique features include: garbage collection, dynamic-typing capability, type safety and advanced built-in types like key-value maps and variable-length arrays. Its standard library also provides us with great features.

The language was developed with a great consideration for systems programming. Rob Pike, Robert Griesemer, and Ken Thompson are behind the development of the Go programming language. Packages are used for the purpose of construction of programs, which leads to an efficient management of dependencies. The executable binaries are generated through the use of the compile and link model, which is very traditional. The language has an in-built support for compilation and it exhibits a very faster rate when it comes to compilation of the programs. Interfaces and Type embedding are supported and its processes are known for their lightweight nature. In Go, statically linked native binaries can be produced without the need for external binaries.

However, some of the features that are common in other programming languages have been deliberately excluded in Go so as to keep it simple. Examples of such features include: the support for assertions, type inheritance, pointer arithmetic, and method or operator overloading.

Chapter 2- Environment Setup

Although there are numerous environments already set up online for the purpose of programming in Go, it is good for you to know how to set your environment up locally. For this to be done, you should have both a text editor and the Go compiler.

Text Editor

This is where your program will be typed. You can choose to use Windows Notepad, Brief, EMACS, Epsilon, OS Edit command, and vim or vi. Of course, the type of operating system you are using and the OS will determine this. Once you have written your program in the text editor, the file will be referred to as the source files, which will have your source code. However, ensure that you save the file in the Go program with a "*.go*" extension.

Before getting deeper into Go programming, you should ensure that you have at least one text editor installed in your system, particularly the one of your choice.

Go Compiler

The source code for a Go program is always in a human readable form. For it to be understood, it has to be compiled so that we can get the machine code. This makes it understandable by the CPU.

The Go distribution is usually available as a binary, which can be installed on Linux, Mac OS X, FreeBSD and the Windows operating system. Both the 32 and 64 bits architectures of the processor are supported.

The first step should involve downloading the installable archive for Go from the official website.

Installation on Mac OS X/Linux/ UNIX and FreeBSD

After the download is completed, extract the archive in the directory *"/usr/local"* and this should create the tree "/usr/local/go". The following command can be used for this purpose:

tar -C /usr/local -xzf go1.4.linux-amd64.tar.gz

Add the directory "/usr/local/go/bin" to the PATH of your environment variable.

Installation on Windows

Identify the MSI file and then use it for installation, following the on screen instructions so as to install the Go tools. For the installation to take effect, just restart any of the command prompts that are opened.

After the installation has been completed, it's a good idea to test whether it was successful or not. Create a new file and give it the name "*myfile.go*". Add the following code to the file:

```
package main

import "fmt"

func main() {

  fmt.Println("Hello, you!")

}
```

To run the file, just execute the following command:

C:\Go_WorkSpace>go run myfile.go

This should give you the following output:

```
Hello, you!
```

Chapter 3- Data Types

In Go programming languages, data types are applied when defining variables and functions. The type of variable that has been defined will determine the amount of space that it will occupy and how the stored bit pattern will be interpreted.

Let us discuss the types that are supported in Go programming language:

Integers

The following are the predefined types of integers in Go:

- uint8 – these are Unsigned 8-bit integers ranging from 0 to 255
- uint16- these are Unsigned 16-bit integers ranging from 0 to 65535
- uint32- these are Unsigned 32-bit integers ranging from 0 to 4294967295
- uint64- these are Unsigned 64-bit integers ranging from 0 to 18446744073709551615
- int8- these are Signed 8-bit
- integers ranging from -128 to 127
- int16- these are Signed 16-bit integers ranging from -32768 to 32767
- int32- these are Signed 32-bit integers ranging from -2147483648 to 2147483647
- int64- these are Signed 64-bit integers ranging from-9223372036854775808 to 9223372036854775807

Floating Types

The following are the predefined floating point types:

- float32- these are 32-bit floating-point numbers (IEEE-754).
- float64- these are 64-bit floating-point numbers (IEEE-754).
- complex64- these are complex numbers having float32 imaginary and real parts.
- complex128- these are complex numbers having float64 imaginary and real parts

Other Numeric Types

These are the numeric types that are implemented with specific sizes. These include the following:

- Byte- this is the same as uint8
- Rune- this is the same as int32
- Uint- this has 32 or 64 bits
- Int- this is same size as a uint
- Uintptr- this an unsigned integer for storing uninterpreted bits of pointer value

Chapter 4- Variables

Variables are used for giving names to storage areas that can be manipulated by our programs. Each variable in Go programming language belongs to a particular type, and this determines the amount of computer memory that it will occupy. This also determines the type of operations that can be performed on the variable.

When defining variables, we can use numbers, letters and the underscore. However, the name of the variable has to begin with a letter or an underscore, but not a number. Go programming language is case sensitive, meaning that there is a great difference between an uppercase and a lowercase letter.

Definition of Variables in Go

Definition of a variable just means informing the compiler of the location and amount of space to preserve for the variable. A variable has to include the data type, and one can specify more than one variable in the same definition. The following syntax is used for doing this:

var variable_list data_type (optional);

Note that the data type has to be valid in Go programming language. Consider the declarations given below, which are valid in Go programming language:

```
var   a, b, c int;
var   x, ch byte;
var  j, wage float32;
z = 56;
```

In the first declaration above, we have declared the variables "*a*", "*b*" and "*c*", which are all of type "*int*". It is also possible for us to initialize variables (assign a value to them) at the time of declaration. In this case, you do not have to state the type of the variable since the compile will automatically know about this from the type of value that you assign to the variable. An equal sign and a constant expression has to be used when declaring constants. The following syntax should be used when declaring constants in Go programming language:

variable_name = value;

Examples of these are shown below:

x = 3, y = 5;

In the above case, we have declared two constants "*x*" and "*y*", with values of 3 and 5 respectively. Although we have not specified that these are integers, the compiler will automatically deduce that from the values that we have assigned to the constants. That is how easy it is. If a variable is not declared as a constant, then its initial value is assigned to be a zero.

Static type declaration

In this way, the compiler is assured that a variable of that type and with that name exists, meaning that it can continue with the process of compilation without the need for further details of the variable. Variable declaration normally has a meaning during compilation, but during the process of linking to your program, the compiler will require the actual variable declaration.

Consider the example given below, which demonstrates how this happens in Go:

package main

```go
import "fmt"

func main() {

  var a float64

  a = 10.0

  fmt.Println(a)

  fmt.Printf("a is of type %T\n", a)

}
```

After execution of the above program, you should get the following as the output:

```
10
a is of type float64
```

In the above example, the function has been declared with a type, and its definition and initialization has been done inside the main function.

Type Inference

When variables have been declared dynamically, a compiler will be needed for the purpose of interpretation of the type of variable. This will depend on the value that has been passed to it.

Consider the example given below showing how this happens in Go:

```
package main

import "fmt"

func main() {

  var a float64 = 10.0

  b := 32

  fmt.Println(a)

  fmt.Println(b)

  fmt.Printf("a is of type %T\n", a)

  fmt.Printf("b is of type %T\n", b)

}
```

After compilation of the above code, you should get the following as the output:

```
32
a is of type float64
b is of type int
```

Mixed variable declaration

We can use type inference so as to declare variables of different types at a Go. Consider the example given below, which shows how this can be done:

package main

import "fmt"

func main() {

  var x, y, name = 5, 10, "Nicholas"

  fmt.Println(x)

  fmt.Println(y)

  fmt.Println(name)

  fmt.Printf("x is of type %T\n", x)

  fmt.Printf("y is of type %T\n", y)

  fmt.Printf("name is of type %T\n", name)

}

After compiling the above program, you will get the following as the output:

```
5
10
Nicholas
x is of type int
y is of type int
name is of type string
```

Chapter 5-Decision Making in Go

With decision making structures in Go, you have to specify a condition or a set of conditions that will be evaluated by the compiler. You also have to specify the statement or statements that are to be executed once the condition has been found to be true, and a statement or statements to be executed once the condition evaluates to false. Let us discuss the decision making statements which are supported in Go programming language.

"if" statement

This statement is made up of a Boolean expression that is then followed by one or more statements. It takes the following syntax:

if(boolean_expression)
{
   /* statement(s) to be execute dif the Boolean expression evaluates to true */

}

Once the condition has evaluated to *"true"*, the set of statements placed inside the *"if"* will be executed. If it evaluates to a *"false"*, then the set of set of statement that appears immediately after the closing curly brace will be executed. Consider the example given below which best describes this:

package main

import "fmt"

func main() {

  /* defining a local variable */

  var x int = 5

```
/* checking the boolean condition by use of if
statement */

if( x < 10 ) {

/* if the condition is true, the following will be
printed*/

    fmt.Printf("x is less than 10\n" )

}

fmt.Printf("The value of x is : %d\n", x)

}
```

After executing the above program, we get the following as the output:

```
x is less than 10
The value of x is : 5
```

"if...else" statement

This is made up of an "*if*" statement, which is then followed by an optional "*else*" statement that is executed when the condition evaluates to false. It takes the following syntax:

```
if(boolean_expression)
{
 /* statement(s) to be executed if the boolean
expression evaluates to true */

}
else
{
 /* statement(s) to be executed if the boolean
expression evaluates to false */

}
```

If the condition evaluates to "*true*", the block for "*if*" will be executed, while if it executes to "*false*", the "*else*" code will be executed. Consider the example given below, which shows how this can be done:

```
package main

import "fmt"

func main() {
```

```go
/* defining a local variable */
var x int = 50;
   /* checking our boolean condition */
if( x < 30 ) {
    /* if the condition is true, the following will be printed */

    fmt.Printf("x is less than 30\n" );
 } else
    /* if the condition is false, the following will be printed*/

    fmt.Printf("x is not less than 30\n" );
 }


 fmt.Printf("The value of x is : %d\n", x);


}
```

After execution of the above code, you should get the following as the output:

```
x is not less than 30
The value of x is : 50
```

"if...else if...else" Statement

This is made up of an "*if*" statement that is then followed by an "*else if...else*", which is very important when it comes to testing of the various conditions. The statement takes the following syntax:

```
if(boolean_expression 1)
{
  /* Will execute when boolean expression 1 evaluates
to true */
}
else if( boolean_expression 2)
-
{
  /* Will execute when none of the above conditions
evaluates to true */
}
```

Consider the example given below, which shows how this statement can be used in Go programming language:

```
package main

import "fmt"

func main() {

  /* defining our local variable */
```

```go
var x int = 50

/* checking the boolean condition */
if( x == 5 ) {

   /* if condition is true, the following will be
printed*/


   fmt.Printf("The value of x is 5\n" )
} else if( x == 10 ) {

   /* if else if condition is true, the following will be
printed */


   fmt.Printf("The value of x is 10\n" )
} else if( x == 20 ) {

   /* if else if condition is true, the following will be
printed */


   fmt.Printf("The value of x is 20\n" )
} else {

   /* if none of conditions evaluates to true */

   fmt.Printf("None of the values was matched\n" )

}

fmt.Printf("The exact value of x is: %d\n", x )
```

```
}
```

Execution of the above program should give you the following output:

```
None of the values was matched
The exact value of x is: 50
```

Nested if statements

In Go, the "*if-else*" statements can be nested. This indicates the "*if*" or "*else if*" statement can be used inside another "*if*" or an "*else if*" statement. This statement takes the following syntax:

```
if( boolean_expression 1)
{
  /* This will execute if the boolean expression 1
evaluates to true */

  if(boolean_expression 2)
  {
    /* will execute if the boolean expression 2 evaluates
to true */

  }
}
```

This statement can be nested in the same way we have done with our previous statement. Consider the example given below, which shows how this statement can be used in Go programming language:

```
package main

import "fmt"

func main() {
```

```
/* defining our local variable */

var x int = 50

var y int = 100

/* checking the boolean condition */

if( x == 50 ) {

    /* if the condition is true, the following will be
checked */


    if( y == 100 ) {

    /* if the condition is true, the following will be
printed*/


    fmt.Printf("The value of x is 50 and y is 100\n" );

    }

}

fmt.Printf("Theexact value of x is : %d\n", x );

fmt.Printf("The exact value of y is : %d\n", y );

}
```

After execution of the above program, you should get the following as the output:

```
The value of x is 50 and y is 100
Theexact value of x is : 50
The exact value of y is : 100
```

switch statement

This statement is used for the purpose of checking for equality of a variable against a list of provided values. The value in this is referred to as *"case"*.

Go programming language supports two types of switch, which include the following:

1. Expression switch- a case has expressions that have to be compared to the value of your switch expression.

2. Type switch- a case has type that will be compared against type of an annotated switch expression.

Expression Switch

This type of switch takes the following syntax in Go programming language:

```
switch(boolean-expression or integral type){
  case boolean-expression or integral type  :
    statement(s);
  case boolean-expression or integral type  :
    statement(s);
  /* the case statements can be of any number */
  default : /* Optional */
    statement(s);
}
```

Consider the example given below, which shows how the switch statement can be used in Go:

```
package main

import "fmt"

func main() {

  /* defining our local variable */

  var grade string = "A"

  var marks int = 95

  switch marks {
```

```
      case 95: grade = "A"

      case 85: grade = "B"

      case 55,65,75 : grade = "C"

      default: grade = "D"

   }

   switch {

      case grade == "A" :

         fmt.Printf("That is excellent!\n" )

      case grade == "B", grade == "C" :

         fmt.Printf("That is good\n" )

      case grade == "D" :

         fmt.Printf("Lucky to have passed!\n" )

      case grade == "F":

         fmt.Printf("You can do better\n" )

      default:

         fmt.Printf("Invalid grade\n" );

   }

   fmt.Printf("The grade is  %s\n", grade );

}
```

Execution of the above program should give you the following output:

```
That is excellent!
The grade is  A
```

Type Switch

This type of "*switch*" statement takes the following syntax in Go programming language:

switch x.(type){

  case type:

    statement(s);

  case type:

    statement(s);

  /* the case statements can be of any number*/

  default: /* Optional */

    statement(s);

}

Consider the following example, which shows how this type of "*switch*" can be implemented:

```go
package main

import "fmt"

func main() {
    var a interface{}
    switch j := a.(type) {
        case nil:
            fmt.Printf("type of a :%T",j)
        case int:
            fmt.Printf("a is an int")
        case float64:
            fmt.Printf("a is a float64")
        case func(int) float64:
            fmt.Printf("a is a func(int)")
        case bool, string:
            fmt.Printf("a is a bool or a string")
        default:
            fmt.Printf("the type is not known")
    }
}
```

Execution of the above program should give you the following output:

```
type of a :
```

Select statement

This statement takes the syntax given below:

select {
  case communication clause :
    statement(s);
  case communication clause :
    statement(s);
  /* the case statements can be of any number */
  default : /* Optional */
    statement(s);
}

You can choose to implement any number of "*case*" statements within the "*select*". The value that is to be compared to, and then a semi colon, should follow each of these cases. The case should take a type of communication channel operation. If the channel operation occurs, the statements that occur after that case will be executed. We do not have to implement a "*break*" in this case. A "*default*" case can be implemented, but this is optional. If this is implemented, it has to appear at the end of your *"select"*. This will help in case none of your *"case"* statements evaluate to true. If a *"default"* has been used, there is no need for the *"break"* statement. The code given below shows how this can be implemented in Go:

```go
package main

import "fmt"

func main() {

  var b1, b2, b3 chan int

  var j1, j2 int

  select {

    case j1 = <-b1:

      fmt.Printf("we have received ", j1, " from b1\n")

    case b2 <- j2:

      fmt.Printf("we sent ", j2, " to b2\n")

    case j3, ok := (<-b3):  // same as: j3, ok := <-b

      if ok {

        fmt.Printf("received ", j3, " from b3\n")

      } else {

        fmt.Printf("b3 has been closed\n")

      }
```

```
     default:

         fmt.Printf("There was no communication\n")

  }

}
```

Execution of the above program should give you the following output:

```
There was no communication
```

Chapter 6- Loops

Sometimes, you may need to execute a particular block of code a number of times. In such a case, the statements will have to be executed in a sequential manner, in which case you will start with the first statement, followed by the second and then the chain continues.

For the purpose of looping, Go provides us with the following looping statements:

"for" Loop

This is a repetition control structure, and it allows you to implement a loop when you are aware of the number of times that you need to execute it. This loop takes the following syntax:

for [condition | (init; condition; increment) | Range]
{
  statement(s);

}

The statements within the loop will have to be executed as long as the condition is met, or evaluates to *"true"*. The step *"init"* has to be executed first, and this is executed only once. Take advantage of this to initialize the control variables for your loop. After that, the *"condition"* has to be evaluated, and if this is found to be true, the body of your loop will have to be executed. If it evaluates to be *"false"*, the body of the loop will be skipped and the statements immediately after the loop will be executed. The part for *"increment"* is used for the purpose of updating any control variables that you have used. However, this is optional as it can be left empty and a semi colon added after the condition. In case you have used the *"range"*, then any value within the range will have to be executed by the loop.

Consider the example given below which shows how this can be done:

```go
package main

import "fmt"

func main() {
  var y int = 10
  var x int
  numbers := [6]int{1, 2, 3, 5}
  /* execution of for loop */
  for x := 0; x < 5; x++ {
    fmt.Printf("value of x: %d\n", x)
  for x < y {
    x++
    fmt.Printf("The value of x: %d\n", x)
    }
  for j,z:= range numbers {
    fmt.Printf("The value of z = %d at %d\n", z,j)
  }
}
```

Execution of the above program will give you the following output:

```
value of x: 0
value of x: 1
value of x: 2
value of x: 3
value of x: 4
The value of x: 1
The value of x: 2
The value of x: 3
The value of x: 4
The value of x: 5
The value of x: 6
The value of x: 7
The value of x: 8
The value of x: 9
The value of x: 10
```

The value of z = 1 at 0

The value of z = 2 at 1

The value of z = 3 at 2

The value of z = 5 at 3

The value of z = 0 at 4

The value of z = 0 at 5

Nested Loops

In Go programming language, one can use one loop inside another loop. The syntax for nesting a *"for"* loop is as shown below:

for [condition | (init; condition; increment) | Range]
{
  for [condition | (init; condition; increment) | Range]

  {
    statement(s);
  }
  statement(s);
}

In the example given below, we have nested a *"for"* loop so as to find the prime numbers that exist between 2 and 100. Here is the code for the example:


```go
package main

import "fmt"

func main() {

  /* defining our local variable*/

  var x, y int

  for x=2; x < 100; x++ {
```

```
for y=2; y <= (x/y); y++ {

  if(x%y==0) {

    break; // if a factor is found, not prime

  }

}

if(y > (x/y)) {

  fmt.Printf("%d is a prime\n", x);

}

}
```

Execution of the above program will give you a list of all the prime numbers between 2 and 100. Below is a section of the output from the code.

```
7 is a prime
11 is a prime
13 is a prime
17 is a prime
19 is a prime
23 is a prime
29 is a prime
31 is a prime
37 is a prime
41 is a prime
43 is a prime
47 is a prime
53 is a prime
59 is a prime
```

Loop Control Statements

Loop control statements always change execution from the normal sequence. Once a particular execution has left a scope, all of the objects created within that scope will be destroyed.

Let us discuss the control statements that are supported in Go programming language.

break statement

This statement is used for terminating a loop and the execution is moved to the next statement contained in the loop. You can also use this statement for the purpose of terminating a *"case"* contained in a *"switch"*.

It takes the following syntax:

break;

Consider the example given below, which shows how this statement can be used:

```
package main
import "fmt"
func main() {
  /*defining our local variable */
  var x int = 20
  /* execution of for loop*/
  for x < 30 {
    fmt.Printf("The value of x: %d\n", x);
```

```
    x++;

    if x > 25 {

        /* use the break statement to terminate the loop
*/

        break;

    }

}
```

The above program should give you the following output after execution:

```
The value of x: 20
The value of x: 21
The value of x: 22
The value of x: 23
The value of x: 24
The value of x: 25
```

continue statement

When this statement is used, the execution of the code inside that loop is skipped and the next iteration is executed. It takes the syntax given below:

continue;

Consider the following example demonstrating how this statement can be used:

```go
package main
import "fmt"
func main() {
  /* defining our local variable */
  var x int = 20
  /* execution of do loop */
  for x < 30 {
    if x == 25 {
      /* skipping the iteration */
      x = x + 1;
      continue;
    }
```

```
fmt.Printf("The value of x is: %d\n", x);

x++;

}

}
```

Execution of the above program gives you the following output:

```
The value of x is: 20
The value of x is: 21
The value of x is: 22
The value of x is: 23
The value of x is: 24
The value of x is: 26
The value of x is: 27
The value of x is: 28
The value of x is: 29
```

As shown in the above output from the program, the value 25 for variable "x" is not part of the output. The reason for this is because it was skipped.

goto statement

This statement in Go is used for providing a conditional jump from a *"goto"* label to a marked statement in the same function.

However, the use of this statement in most programming languages has been discouraged since, when used, it becomes hard for us to know how the flow control of a program has been done.

The statement takes the following syntax:

goto label;

..

.

label: statement;

The following example demonstrates how this statement can be used in Go programming language:

package main

import "fmt"

func main() {

  /* defining our local variable */

```
var x int = 20

/* execution  of do loop */

LOOP: for x < 30 {

   if x == 25 {

     /* skipping the iteration */

     x = x + 1

     goto LOOP

   }

   fmt.Printf("The value of x: %d\n", x)

   x++

 }

}
```

A successful execution of the above program gives the following output:

```
The value of x: 20
The value of x: 21
The value of x: 22
The value of x: 23
The value of x: 24
The value of x: 26
The value of x: 27
The value of x: 28
The value of x: 29
```

Infinite Loop

This is a type of loop in which condition will never evaluate to a false. Traditionally, the "*for*" loop was used for this purpose. The three expressions that form the "*for*" loop are not needed, meaning that you can choose to pass a "*true*" to it or just leave it being empty. This is demonstrated in the example given below:

```go
package main
import "fmt"
func main() {
 for true {
    fmt.Printf("The loop will be executed forever.\n");
 }
}
```

In the absence of the conditional expressional, it is assumed that it is true. Although the conditional should be stated, the increment and the initialization can be specified.

Chapter 7-Go Functions

A function is simply a set of statements that have been grouped together for the sake of performing the same task. In Go, the *"main()"* function is used in all programs and one is free to define other additional functions.

You can take advantage of functions to subdivide your code into specific sections. Declaration of a function means telling the compiler about the name of the function, the return type and the list of parameters. Definition of a function refers to providing the actual body of the function. There are numerous functions in the Go standard library that you can feel free to call.

Function Definition

The following syntax is used for definition of functions in Go:

func function_name([parameter list])
[return_types]
{
  function body

}

When defining functions in Go, we should have the following necessary parts of a function:

1. func- this is used for starting the declaration of the function.

2. Function Name- represents the actual name of the function. When calling a function, a value has to be passed to the parameter.

3. Parameters- this acts like a placeholder. This should be the actual value of the parameter.

4. Return Type- this should be the type of data which the parameters of the function should return. Some functions will perform the desired operations without having to return any value.

5. Function Body- this should be made up of a number of statements that will define the purpose of the function.

Consider the example program given below, which shows a sample function in Go:

/* A function to return the maximum between two numbers */

```
func max(number1, number2 int) int
{
  /* declaration  of a local variable */
  result int
  if (number1 > number2) {
    result = number1
  } else {
    result = number2
  }
  return result
}
```

In the above example, we have used the "*max()*" function, which should return the largest number between the two numbers that have been passed to the function.

Calling a Function

During the creation of a function in Go, you have to define what the function is expected to do. For the function to be used, you will have to call it so as to perform the task that you need it to perform.

To call the function, you have to use its name along with the necessary parameters. Also, if you expect the function to return a value, you can choose to store the returned value. Consider the example given below:

```go
package main
import "fmt"
func main() {
  /* definition of the local variable */
  var x int = 50
  var y int = 100
  var ret int
  /* call the function to obtain the max value */
  ret = max(x, y)
  fmt.Printf( "The max value is : %d\n", ret )
}
/* a function which will return the maximum between
two numbers */

func max(number1, number2 int) int {
  /* declaration of a local variable */
  var result int
  if (number1 > number2) {
    result = number1
```

```
  } else {
    result = number2
  }
  return result
}
```

Once the above program has been compiled, the following should be observed as the output:

```
The max value is : 100
```

It is also possible to return several values from just a single function. Consider the following example, which shows how this can be done in Go:

package main

```
package main
import "fmt"
func swap(a, b string) (string, string) {
  return b, a
}
func main() {
  x, y := swap("Nicholas", "John")
  fmt.Println(x, y)

}
```

After compilation of the above programs, you should get the following output:

-We have used the *"swap()"*function so as to swap the order of the two names.

Function Arguments

If a function is expected to accept arguments, variables will have to be declared that are expected to accept the values of our arguments. The variables are usually the formal parameters of our function.

During a function call, there are two ways that you can pass arguments to it:

Call by Value

In this method, the actual values of the parameters have to be copied to the formal parameters of the function. This is the default method that is used in Go for the purpose of passing arguments.

This can be demonstrated by use of the *"swap()"* method as shown below:

```
package main
import "fmt"
func main() {
  /* defining our local variable */
  var x int = 50
  var y int = 100
```

```
    fmt.Printf("Before swap, the value of x : %d\n", x )
    fmt.Printf("Before swap, the value of y : %d\n", y )
    /* calling the function for swapping the values */
    swap(x, y)
    fmt.Printf("After swap, the value of x : %d\n", x )
    fmt.Printf("After swap, the value of y : %d\n", y )
}
func swap(a, b int) int {
    var temp int
    temp = a /* will save the value of the value of a */
    a = b   /* putting a into b */
    b = temp /* putting temp into b */
    return temp;
}
```

After compilation of the above program, we should get the following as the output:

```
Before swap, the value of x : 50
Before swap, the value of y : 100
After swap, the value of x : 50
After swap, the value of y : 100
```

Although the values had been changed inside the function, they have not changed, and that is what happens in Go functions.

Chapter 8- Structures

A structure is a data type used in Go for holding values of different types, and it is user defined.

During the definition of structures, one has to use the keywords *"type"* and struct". The struct statement takes the following syntax:

type struct_variable_type struct {
  member;
  member;
  ...
  member;
}

After the definition of the structure type, we can use it for definition of variables of that type using the syntax given below:

variable_name := structure_variable_type {value1, value2 ...valuen}

How to Access Structure Members

The operator (.) is used for the purpose of accessing the members of a structure. Consider the example given below, which shows how this can be done:

```go
package main
import "fmt"
type StudyMaterials struct {
  title string
  author string
  subject string
  material_id int
}
func main() {
  var Material1 StudyMaterials
  var Material2 StudyMaterials
  Material1.title = "Programming in Go"
  Material1.author = "Nicholas Musembi"
  Material1.subject = "How to program in Go"
Material1.material_id = 2389708
  /* material 2 specification */
  Material2.title = "C# Programming"
  Material2.author = "Nicholas Samuel"
  Material2.subject = "How to program in C#"
  Material2.material_id = 2389712
  /* printing Material1 info */
  fmt.Printf( " Material 1 title : %s\n", Material1.title)
  fmt.Printf( " Material 1 author : %s\n",
Material1.author)
  fmt.Printf( " Material 1 subject : %s\n",
Material1.subject)
```

```
fmt.Printf( " Material 1 material_id : %d\n",
Material1. material_id)

/* printing Material2 info */
fmt.Printf( " Material 2 title : %s\n", Material2.title)
fmt.Printf( " Material 2 author : %s\n",
Material2.author)
fmt.Printf( " Material 2 subject : %s\n",
Material2.subject)
fmt.Printf( " Material 2 material_id : %d\n",
Material2. material_id)

}
```

Execution of the above program should give you the following
as the output:

```
Material 1 title : Programming in Go
Material 1 author : Nicholas Musembi
Material 1 subject : How to program in Go
Material 1 material_id : 2389708
Material 2 title : C# Programming
Material 2 author : Nicholas Samuel
Material 2 subject : How to program in C#
Material 2 material_id : 2389712
```

Structures as Function Arguments

A structure can be passes as a function argument just as variables and pointers are passed. In such a case, the structure variables can be accessed in the same way as we have done previously. Consider the example given below, which shows how this is done:

package main

```go
package main
import "fmt"
type StudyMaterials struct {
  title string
  author string
  subject string
  material_id int
}
func main() {
  var Material1 StudyMaterials
  var Material2 StudyMaterials
  /* material 1 specification */
  Material1.title = "Programming in Go"
  Material1.author = "Nicholas Musembi"
  Material1.subject = "How to program in Go"
  Material1.material_id = 2389708
  /* material 2 specification */
  Material2.title = "C# Programming"
  Material2.author = "Nicholas Samuel"
  Material2.subject = "How to program in C#"
```

```go
Material2.material_id = 2389712
/* print Material1 info */
printMaterial(Material1)
/* print Material2 info */
printMaterial (Material2)
}
func printMaterial( material StudyMaterials )
{
  fmt.Printf( "Material title : %s\n", material.title);
  fmt.Printf( " Material author : %s\n",
material.author);
  fmt.Printf( " Material subject : %s\n",
material.subject);
  fmt.Printf( " Material material_id : %d\n",
material.material_id);
}
```

Execution of the above code will give you details of the study materials similar to what we did in our previous example.

Pointers to Structures

For you to define pointers to structures, use the syntax given below:

var struct_pointer *StudyMaterials

Consider the example given below, which shows how this can be implemented:

```
package main
import "fmt"
type StudyMaterials struct {
  title string
  author string
  subject string
  material_id int
}
func main() {
  var Material1 StudyMaterials
  var Material2 StudyMaterials
  /* material 1 specification */
  Material1.title = "Programming in Go"
  Material1.author = "Nicholas Musembi"
  Material1.subject = "How to program in Go"
  Material1.material_id = 2389708
  /* material 2 specification */
  Material2.title = "C# Programming"
  Material2.author = "Nicholas Samuel"
  Material2.subject = "How to Program in C#"
  Material2.material_id = 2389712
```

```
  /* print Material1 info */
  printMaterial(&Material1)
  /* print Material2 info */
  printMaterial(&Material2)
}
func printMaterial( material *StudyMaterials )
{
 fmt.Printf( "Material title : %s\n", material.title);
 fmt.Printf( "Material author : %s\n",
material.author);
 fmt.Printf( "Material subject : %s\n",
material.subject);
 fmt.Printf( "Material material_id : %d\n",
material.material_id);
}
```

That is it.

Chapter 9- Interfaces

This is another type of data structure in Go that provides us with method signatures. The "Struct" data type is used for the purpose of implementing the interfaces so as to have definitions of methods for method signature of interfaces.

Consider the example given below:

```
package main

import (

  "fmt"

  "math"

)

/* defining the interface */

type Object interface {

  area() float64

}

/* defining a circle */

type Circle struct {

  a,b,radius float64

}
```

```go
/* defining a rectangle */
type Rectangle struct {
  width, height float64
}
/* defining the method for the circle */
func(circle Circle) area() float64 {
  return math.Pi * circle.radius * circle.radius
}
/* defining a method for the rectangle */
func(rectangle Rectangle) area() float64 {
  return rectangle.width * rectangle.height
}
/* defining a method for the object */
func getArea(object Object) float64 {
  return object.area()
}
func main() {
  circle := Circle{a:0,b:0,radius:6}
  rect := Rectangle {width:5, height:15}
  fmt.Printf("The circle area: %f\n",getArea(circle))
  fmt.Printf("The rectangle area: %f\n",getArea(rect))
```

}\

Execution of the above program should give you the following output:

```
The circle area: 113.097336
The rectangle area: 75.000000
```

Chapter 10- Concurrency

Large programs in Go are always made up of sub-programs. These should be run together, a technique referred to as *"concurrency"*. Go uses *"Routines"* and *"Channels"* so as to support concurrency.

GoRoutines

This represents a function with the capability of running concurrently with other functions. It is created by use of the *"go"* keyword, which is followed by invocation of the function. This is shown below:

```
package main
import "fmt"
func myFunction(x int) {
 for j := 0; j < 10; j++
   fmt.Println(x, ":", j)
 }
}
func main() {
 go myFunction(0)
 var input string
 fmt.Scanln(&input)
}
```

We have implemented two routines in the above program. The first one is implicit, and represents the main function. The second goroutine happens after calling the "go f(0)".

Goroutines are very lightweight, meaning that it is possible for us to create thousands of them. If we need to modify the program so that it can run 5 routines, we can do it as follows:

```
func main() {
 for j := 0; j < 5; j++ {
   go f(j)
 }
 var input string
 fmt.Scanln(&input)
}
```

You might have noticed that after running the above program, the goroutines will be executed in an order other than doing it simultaneously. Let us use "rand.Intn" and "time.Sleep" so as to add some delay to our function:

```
package main
import (
 "fmt"
 "time"
 "math/rand"
)
func myFunction(x int) {
 for j := 0; j < 5; j++ {
   fmt.Println(x, ":", j)
```

```go
    amt := time.Duration(rand.Intn(250))
    time.Sleep(time.Millisecond * amt)
  }
}
func main() {
 for j := 0; j < 10; j++ {
  go myFunction(j)
 }
 var input string
 fmt.Scanln(&input)
}
```

The "*f*" will print out the numbers 0 to 5, and it will take between 0 and 250 milliseconds for each number to be printed. It is now possible for the goroutines to run simultaneously.

Channels

In Go, channels can be used for the purpose of establishing communication between two goroutines, as well as synchronization of these. Consider the example given below which shows a Go program that makes use of channels:

```
package main
import (
 "fmt"
 "time"
func pingerFunction(c chan string) {
 for j := 0; ; j++ {
   c <- "ping"
 }
}
func pingerFunction(c chan string) {
 for {
   msg := <- c

   fmt.Println(msg)
   time.Sleep(time.Second * 1)
 }
}
func main() {
 var c chan string = make(chan string)
 go pingerFunction(c)
 go pingerFunction(c)
 var input string
 fmt.Scanln(&input)
}
```

The above program will run forever, and for you to stop it from execution, you will have to hit the enter key. The channel type is represented by use of the keyword *"chan"*, which should be followed by the things that are to be passed through the channel. The left arrow (<-) is used for the purpose of sending and receiving messages on our channel.

When a channel like the one created about is used, the two go routines are synchronized. Let us try to add another sender to our program and then observe what will happen. The following function should be added:

```
func ponger(c chan string) {
 for j := 0; ; j++ {
  c <- "pong"
 }
}
```

The *"main"* should then be modified as follows:

```
func main() {
 var ch chan string = make(chan string)
 go pinger(ch)
 go ponger(ch)
 go printer(ch)
 var input string
 fmt.Scanln(&input)
}
```

The program will then print *"ping"* and *"pong"* and it will take turns when doing this.

Channel Direction

It is possible for us to specify the direction on our channel so that it can be restricted to either sending or receiving. Consider the example given below, which shows how the signature for the pinger function can be modified:

func pinger(c chan<- string)

The "*c*" can be send to only. If we attempt to receive from the "*c*", we will get a compile error. The printer can then be changed to the following:

func printer(c <-chan string)

If a channel lacks the above restrictions, it is referred to as a bi-directional channel. This one can be passed to any function that takes receive-only and send-only channels, but the reverse will not be true.

Select

This is a special statement in Go programming language that works like the *"switch"* statement, but this time for channels only. The example given below shows how this can be used in Go:

```go
func main() {
 ch1 := make(chan string)
 ch2 := make(chan string)
 go func() {
  for {
   ch1 <- "from 1"
   time.Sleep(time.Second * 2)
  }
 }()
 go func() {
  for {
   ch2 <- "from 2"
   time.Sleep(time.Second * 3)
  }
 }()
 go func() {
  for {
   select {
   case msg1 := <- ch1:
    fmt.Println(msg1)
   case msg2 := <- ch2:
    fmt.Println(msg2)
   }
  }
```

```
}()
var input string
fmt.Scanln(&input)
}
```

The statement *"select"* is always used for the purpose of implementation of a timeout. The following code best describes this:

```
select {
case msg1 := <- b1:
 fmt.Println("Message 1 is", msg1)
case msg2 := <- b2
 fmt.Println("Message 2 is", msg2)
case <- time.After(time.Second):
 fmt.Println("timeout")
}
```

The "time.After" will create a channel and then the current time will be sent on it after a particular duration. The code given below best describes this:

```
select {
case msg1 := <- b1:
 fmt.Println("Message 1 is", msg1)
case msg2 := <- b2:
 fmt.Println("Message 2 is", msg2)
case <- time.After(time.Second):
 fmt.Println("timeout")
default:
 fmt.Println("nothing is ready")
```

```
}
```

The default case will immediately happen if none of our channels is found to be ready.

Buffered Channels

When you are creating your channel, you can pass a second parameter to your make function. The following syntax can be used for doing this:

b := make(chan int, 1)

With the above code, a buffered channel will be created with a capacity of 1. The channels are always synchronous, meaning that the channel's sides will wait until the other side becomes ready for transmission.

Chapter 11- Slices

These are used for the purpose of abstracting arrays. They provide many utility functions that are required on an array.

Slice Definition

These can be defined as arrays without having to specify the size or use the keyword "make" so as to create a new one. This is done as shown below:

var nums []int /* a slice for unspecified size */
/* nums == []int{0,0,0,0,0}*/
nums = make([]int,5,5) /* a slice having a length of 5 and a capacity of 5*/

cap() and len() functions

The "*len()*" function is used for the purpose of returning the elements contained in the slice. The function "*cap()*" is used for returning the capacity of the slice in terms of the number of elements that it can accommodate. The example given below describes how a slice can be implemented:

```
package main
import "fmt"
func main() {
  var nums = make([]int,10,20)
  printSlice(nums)
}
func printSlice(y []int){
  fmt.Printf("len=%d cap=%d slice=%v\n",len(y),cap(y),y)
}
```

The above program should return the following output:

```
len=10 cap=20 slice=[0 0 0 0 0 0 0 0 0 0]
```

Nil slice

If the declaration of a slice is done with no inputs, then the default setting is that it is initialized as nil. The length and capacity is 0. Consider the example given below:

```go
package main

import "fmt"

func main() {

 var nums []int

  printSlice(nums)

 if(nums == nil){

  fmt.Printf("The slice is nil")

 }

}

func printSlice(y []int){

 fmt.Printf("len=%d cap=%d slice=%v\n",len(y),cap(y),y)

}
```

The above program will give the following output when compiled:

```
len=0 cap=0 slice=[]
The slice is nil
```

sub-slicing

With slices, you can specify the upper-bound and lower-bound so as to come up with a sub-slice. Consider the following example that best describes this:

package main

import "fmt"

func main() {

  /* creating a slice */

  nums := []int{10,11,12,13,14,15,16,17,18}

  printSlice(nums)

   /* printing the original slice */

  fmt.Println("numbers ==", nums)

    /* printing the sub slice beginning from index 1 to the index 4*/

  fmt.Println("nums[1:4] ==", nums[1:4])

  /* When the lower bound is absent, it implies 0*/

```go
fmt.Println("nums[:3] ==", nums[:3])

/* a missing upper bound is an implication of len(s)*/

fmt.Println("nums[4:] ==", nums[4:])

nums1 := make([]int,0,5)

printSlice(nums1

  nums2 := nums[:2]

printSlice(nums2)

/* printing the sub slice beginning from index 2 to index 5*/

num3 := nums[2:5]

printSlice(num3)

func printSlice(y []int){

fmt.Printf("len=%d cap=%d slice=%v\n",len(y),cap(y),y)

}
```

Execution of the above program will give you the following output:

```
len=9 cap=9 slice=[10 11 12 13 14 15 16 17 18]
numbers == [10 11 12 13 14 15 16 17 18]
nums[1:4] == [11 12 13]
nums[:3] == [10 11 12]
nums[4:] == [14 15 16 17 18]
len=0 cap=5 slice=[]
len=2 cap=9 slice=[10 11]
len=3 cap=7 slice=[12 13 14]
```

copy() append() functions

The "*append()*" function can be used for the purpose of increasing the capacity of a slice. The function "*copy()*" is used for copying the elements of a source slice to your destination slice. Consider the example given below, which best demonstrates how this can be done:

package main

import "fmt"

func main() {

  var nums []int

  printSlice(nums)

  /* appending allows nil slice */

  nums = append(nums, 0)

  printSlice(nums

  /* adding one element to the slice*/

  nums = append(nums, 1)

```go
    printSlice(nums)

    /* adding more than one element each time*/

    nums = append(nums, 12,13,14)

    printSlice(nums)

    /* creating a slice nums1 with double capacity of
the earlier slice*/


    nums1 := make([]int, len(nums), (cap(nums))*2)

    /* copying the content of the numbers to nums1 */

    copy(nums1,nums)

    printSlice(nums1)
}
func printSlice(y[]int){
  fmt.Printf("len=%d cap=%d
slice=%v\n",len(y),cap(y),y)
}
```

Execution of the above program will give you the following output:

```
len=0 cap=0 slice=[]
len=1 cap=1 slice=[0]
len=2 cap=2 slice=[0 1]
len=5 cap=6 slice=[0 1 12 13 14]
len=5 cap=12 slice=[0 1 12 13 14]
```

Conclusion

We have come to the conclusion of this book. Go is a very easy programming language that anyone can easily learn to program in. The program was developed in such a way that its users can accomplish more while using less code. The language has a number of features unique to those offered in other programming languages, which allow users to create amazing applications. To program in Go, you have to begin by preparing the necessary environmental requirements. You should have an editor and the Go compiler. However, you can take advantage of free online environments to program in Go.

The programming language supports basic features such as use of variables and data of various types. Decision making statements are highly supported in Go and you can take advantage of these to control the flow of your program. Loops, which are structures for controlling the execution of programs, are also supported. You are also able to create functions in Go. You can choose to organize your code into different parts, each made up of a function. Go programming language also supports the use of structures and you can take advantage of these to store data of different types. Structures can be used together with pointers in Go programming language. Instead of using arrays, Go allows you to use slices, which are more advanced. In fact, appending elements to it can increase the size of a slice. We hope this book has been useful to you!

2

3   Redistribution and use in source and binary forms, with or without

4   modification, are permitted provided that the following conditions are

5   met:

6

7   * Redistributions of source code must retain the above copyright

8   notice, this list of conditions and the following disclaimer.

9   * Redistributions in binary form must reproduce the above

10   copyright notice, this list of conditions and the following disclaimer

11   in the documentation and/or other materials provided with the

12   distribution.

13   * Neither the name of Google Inc. nor the names of its

14 contributors may be used to endorse or promote products derived from

15 this software without specific prior written permission.

16

17 THIS SOFTWARE IS PROVIDED BY THE COPYRIGHT HOLDERS AND CONTRIBUTORS

18 "AS IS" AND ANY EXPRESS OR IMPLIED WARRANTIES, INCLUDING, BUT NOT

19 LIMITED TO, THE IMPLIED WARRANTIES OF MERCHANTABILITY AND FITNESS FOR

20 A PARTICULAR PURPOSE ARE DISCLAIMED. IN NO EVENT SHALL THE COPYRIGHT

21 OWNER OR CONTRIBUTORS BE LIABLE FOR ANY DIRECT, INDIRECT, INCIDENTAL,

22 SPECIAL, EXEMPLARY, OR CONSEQUENTIAL DAMAGES (INCLUDING, BUT NOT

23 LIMITED TO, PROCUREMENT OF SUBSTITUTE GOODS OR SERVICES; LOSS OF USE,

24 DATA, OR PROFITS; OR BUSINESS INTERRUPTION) HOWEVER CAUSED AND ON ANY

25 THEORY OF LIABILITY, WHETHER IN CONTRACT, STRICT LIABILITY, OR TORT

26 (INCLUDING NEGLIGENCE OR OTHERWISE) ARISING IN ANY WAY OUT OF THE USE

27 OF THIS SOFTWARE, EVEN IF ADVISED OF THE POSSIBILITY OF SUCH DAMAGE.